Letting Go of the Façade

Using Your Mental Health Journey to Live a More Authentic Life By Rachel George

RACHEL GEORGE

Publishing Services provided by Paper Raven Books LLC Printed in the United States of America.

First Printing, 2023

Paperback ISBN= 979-8-8582-4401-1
Hardback ISBN= 978-1-3999-6033-5

Professional review

A very good read. Very thought provoking and a stripped back step by step guide on how to become a more authentic version of yourself. I enjoyed the reflection questions at the end of each chapter as this brought space for grounding, exploration of thoughts, and exposure to a part of self that may not have been previously considered.

~Georgina Brandon
(PgDIP MBACP Counsellor and Psychotherapist)

Contents

1. A mental health crisis

Disclaimer: I am not qualified to provide medical advice. If you are someone who experiences mental health issues, a doctor should always be consulted in order to determine the most appropriate form of treatment.

My nights consisted of dreading the next day. My days consisted of waiting for them to finish. I was spending the majority of my time in a job that I didn't have the energy to do. I was aiming to fake it until I made it, but I had no notion of what 'making it' would feel like. My actions day-to-day had no bearing on my genuine interests. If I had more money, I would have been living a completely different life. Put simply, I was headed for burn-out. It would not be until the lockdowns during COVID-19 when I could step back and be truly honest with myself. I was not living a life that fulfilled me or offered me a sense of purpose. As I look back now, I know this was a turning point for me. I made the decision to break with inauthentic patterns in myself and in my life more broadly. By that, I mean breaking with a life that I shaped to meet the expectations of others rather than the needs and wants of myself. The COVID-19 pandemic seems to have triggered this same realisation in many other people around the globe. Some of us were fortunate to have had more time for ourselves to reflect as a result of the pandemic and the enforced lockdowns. What was a very uneasy and anxious time also helped some of us to feel as though a light had been switched on in a dirty room, illuminating the places that hadn't been cleaned in a while—if ever.

The pandemic collided with an era defined in large part by a 'mental health crisis.' We're not sure if there are more people suffering with mental health illnesses, or if the development in research and public awareness has led to an increase in diagnoses. Either way, there are high rates of people suffering today. In 2022, the WHO said that one in every eight people in the world live with a mental disorder (World Health Organization, 2022). That is close to 1 billion people… 1 billion! We also have to factor in that the likelihood of someone receiving a mental health diagnosis depends on the quality of the healthcare system. Since the standard of healthcare systems will vary from country to country, this could mean that some countries are going to have more success in accurately diagnosing patients than others. In other words, it could be that more than one in eight people struggle with mental illness.

I wonder why the prevalence of mental illness is so high. There are a whole host of potential causes. One of the most talked about is trauma. Trauma does not necessarily have to be a significant event. It can also be a prolonged time period during which needs are not being met. If you can recall something that makes you angry, sad, or just want to turn a blind eye, that is trauma. An example of my own trauma is my parents being very exhausted and sometimes withdrawn during my childhood, which was largely outside of their control because they were experiencing severe mental health issues at a time when there was little understanding about mental health. It would make me less open and less trusting of people, because these were my responses to the circumstances.

Trauma is not the only big cause that could account for the prevalence of mental illness in today's world. There is another one, namely rushing, which gets overlooked. I think it's easy enough to dismiss because it seems so small or trivial, but its impact can be disproportionate. Think about how often you're rushing to miss the red traffic light, rushing to get that deadline met, rushing to get home so you can finally wind down. We are human 'beings', yet so many of us are trying to be human 'doers'. I led a life of constant rush, where the aim was to get things done so that I could have more time to relax on evenings and weekends. It meant that my mind was constantly wanting to be somewhere else, and so I was not accepting of the present moment. We are not wired to be productive all the time. I believe that for as long as we don't consciously make an effort to have more 'being' time, our suffering will continue.

Although I'm not an expert in mental health, I do want to share my own experience of tackling mental health issues. I was a very dissociated person during my adolescent years and early adulthood, until COVID-19 hit. This meant that everything in my life was on pause, and I had the time and the headspace to start working on my mental health. Just recently, I also experienced a period of acute psychosis. I feel it's necessary to introduce these struggles with reference to my childhood. I explain it all from a self-reflecting perspective in an attempt to demonstrate the power of self-reflection and how it enabled me to see my own dysfunctional behaviours. I go on to share effective tools which have significantly improved my mental health. I love science and so share the key bits of research that corroborate the effectiveness of these tools. It's the tools shared within this book that have enabled me to progress from being a dissociated, numb person to someone who is more emotional but far more connected to the world around me.

An effective way to create change is to share stories and our own unique interpretations of the world. Sometimes we have to hear things a different way if they are to resonate with us, and what works for one person won't work for another. A common critique of self-help books today is that they share nothing new. I see two sides. One is that, as generations go by, we forget things. We can't just have one book published and be comfortable that it's out there and so doesn't need to be said again. Messages need reiterating to remind the newer generations. The other side is that self-help books will have consistent themes. It's the day you don't have to read another self-help book but feel comfortable with your own resources that you've progressed. I hope this book will help you develop a relationship with yourself that puts you in touch with your inner resources, as well as the red flags when there's a need for external help.

It is my sincere hope that the inner and outer resources I've gathered in this book will prove as useful for you as they did for me.

2. Nervous system regulation

"Ultimately, we gain mastery over emotions by controlling the body." -(Millman, 2010)

Throughout my late teens and early 20s, I was working and studying full-time. Where I would be located for work differed week to week. I was pretty much living out of my suitcase because of the extensive travel. In the meantime, I had limited time to switch off because my weekends would often entail revising for my next exam. All this work and study was to enable me to qualify as a chartered accountant. That was the career path I had chosen to pursue. However, my adrenaline and cortisol levels were consistently high, and I found it difficult to relax in the face of deadlines around every corner. There were many situations where people just seemed calmer than me, and I couldn't understand why. I remember feeling familiar with this type of dynamic as early as going on my first day trip with my friends and without any adults. I was so stressed about potentially getting the wrong train or some other problem. My struggle to relax would bring about other symptoms over the long-term like fatigue, muddled thinking, worrying, low mood, and anxiety. To address these symptoms, I created a routine that not only helped me to burn energy but made me feel like I accomplished something. I would feel more confident. Specifically, strengthening the mind-body connection would help me to do what's known as regulating the nervous system.

Traditionally, it's been accepted that mental health disorders are caused by chemical imbalances in the brain. Those diagnosed may be prescribed medication and make some lifestyle improvements to help ease symptoms, but the diagnosis may be with them for the rest of their life. However, recent developments in science are starting to suggest that chemical imbalances in the brain may only be a by-product of what the real potential issue is. That issue is a dysregulated nervous system (MindHealth360, n.d.). Before I go on to explain what this is, I want to highlight why this information could change the direction of the mental health movement. The cause of a dysregulated nervous system for many of us is treatable.

As a species we've moved from being cavemen to living in the modern world. Yet we still experience the same threat response. Rather than being triggered by something truly life-threatening such as a tiger, it's more often triggered by those small but frequent pressures of modern-day life. Our brains haven't learnt that, in most instances, our physical body is not under threat, because the modern world is still relatively new to us as a species. Anything new is considered a potential threat. That's one of the big roles of the brain, to be on the lookout for potential threats to survival.

Some modern-day pressures can seem trivial to us at first, but they build up and up when a person does not give themselves the opportunity to exit the threat response fully. I used to spend every morning snoozing my alarm multiple times, making it so I had to rush to get ready in order to arrive at work on time. Compare those days to the days that did not begin with a rush. There was a significant difference in my energy, temperament, and resilience. This is how a nervous system can become dysregulated. Even when a person is supposedly relaxing, there will be symptoms. This can show up as sleep issues, poor eating habits, and mood swings. Chances are that a lot of us don't give ourselves the opportunity to regulate the nervous system because of the following:

a) We may not realise we need to whilst we are in autopilot mode and lack awareness, and

b) We may not give ourselves the time because of the need to prioritise other more immediate responsibilities.

Do any of the following symptoms resonate with you (per NHS)? If so, consider consulting a doctor. Whatever the cause, incorporating stretches and other exercises that release tensions in your routine can always help to, at the very least, ease these symptoms.

- Headaches
- Fatigue
- Muddled thinking
- Worrying
- Low mood
- Anxiety
- Insomnia

I did search for data to help provide insight on what percentage of people have a dysregulated nervous system, and it's not something there seems to be a straight answer for. However, if we consider that there are one in eight people diagnosed with a mental disorder, then I would hypothesise that at the very least one in eight people have a dysregulated nervous system. In fact, I would not be surprised if we all have degrees of a dysregulated nervous system because of the fast-paced world. If this is the case, then it could be that having a dysregulated nervous system has become normalised. How could this become acceptable? Perhaps it's seen to keep the economy moving. It enables short-term corporate incentives and projects to be accomplished. It's what enables us as cogs in the capitalist machine to keep moving.

However, in the long run, it only seems to run a person down.

If our body is relaxed, then we are more likely to have a regulated nervous system. If our mind is relaxed, our body is relaxed. The body and the mind can be seen as reflections of one another. I will refer to the relationship of mind and body as the mind-body connection, a term that's likely familiar to some readers. The most important insight that the concept of the mind-body connection provides is that we have to work on mind and body simultaneously to arrive at a state of stability and health. For better or worse, it is a two-way cycle, and so we have to treat both. Treating both mind and body will enhance their connection and make us feel safe in ourselves.

A fundamental part of my daily routine to regulate my nervous system is doing stretches. Research has shown that stretching reduces stress hormone levels. This helped me to become more conscious of where there were tensions in my body. In addition to stretches, a turning point for me was seeing a chiropractor and learning how to have good posture. Those with depression are more likely to have a head tilted downward and shoulders shrugging forward. That was my stance. At first, when attempting good posture, I struggled to breathe correctly from my diaphragm. I spent 10 minutes each day practising diaphragm breathing, lying on my back with my knees up, and that would help enable my mind to learn how to breathe properly. There's a whole host of exercises or regimes that can be used to regulate the nervous system. A recent trendy one is cold water therapy.

The result of adopting these regimens was a more regulated nervous system. I became a more relaxed person, and this showed through the depth of sleep I was having. I found it to be powerful to have my body tell my mind that things are okay, rather than have my mind tell my mind. Often, I'd try to think myself out of problems or situations, and that could be never-ending. There are some things you can't think yourself out of.

This could perhaps be a root issue with a common misconception that, if we achieve a certain goal or obtain a material item we've wanted, we will be happy. Actually, what often happens is a short period of feeling relaxed, and then it's not long until we look for the next thing.

What if we could extend that physical feeling of relaxation and bring it into our daily lives, no matter the external circumstances? I believe that deep breath of relief we take, or satisfaction we have in achieving a goal, is actually the feeling that we often chase. It is something we can learn to bring into our lives daily such that we don't have to chase any longer.

A dysregulated nervous system would not mean something is wrong with us. It's actually the opposite. It means our brain is effectively sending signals to the nervous system that there is a threat. The brain then switches off and the body takes over. The brain doesn't recognise that its definition of a threat is far too broad. That doesn't mean anything is wrong with the brain. It just highlights that we are still wired like monkeys in a world that so often requests us to perform like robots. We have the capacity to reduce the amount of time we spend being dysregulated, and therefore we ultimately have the capability of improving our mental well-being.

Reflection question:

What are you feeling right now?

Stand up and stretch. Reach your arms as high as they will go. What do you feel as you stretch? Where can you feel the tension in your body? What can you do to release that tension?

3. Neuroplasticity

I contend that a mental health crisis is emerging because we live in a time that is much more fast-paced and instant than anything our biology had to adapt to in the natural world. We can change our behaviour to cope with this pace in a way that exacerbates dysfunction, or we can do the opposite. When we develop good habits for ourselves and make nervous system regulation a priority, our brains create new neural pathways to mirror these habits. We are not stuck wholly with the mindset developed during childhood. Through a process known as neuroplasticity, the brain is capable of rewiring its connections throughout adulthood in response to new experiences (Hampton, 2019). This means we have the power to change our brain structure. The nervous system reacts to the brain and the signals that are sent to it.

Therefore, we need to work on our mind and re-teach it what situations are safe and not safe. We have the power to alter the signal usually sent to the nervous system in triggering situations. This adds an element of scientific proof of the phrase, 'you can achieve anything you put your mind to'.

There was a brain-imaging study that found London cab drivers all had something in common. The area of the brain that relates to spatial awareness has far stronger neural connections when compared to the average person (Culture, 2013). This is because London cab drivers are required to memorise the map of London. It's likely that this requirement resulted in more activity in the corresponding part of the brain. This is an example of the power of neuroplasticity and the brain's ability to adapt.

There is no such thing as a quick fix when it comes to teaching our brains that a situation is safe, such as that anxiety you wish you didn't feel ahead of a night out, or during a plane landing, for instance. In order to create new wired pathways in the brain, repetition is needed. Repetition is key when it comes to self-healing. This is why to actually make lasting change after reading this book, practising habits is fundamental. Note that I say 'practising' and not 'completing'. It's the effort that matters, and there will be days you can't be bothered. On those days, self-compassion is an absolute necessity. It will help you to conserve energy to pick yourself back up when you are ready.

I learnt the value of neuroplasticity when I incorporated exercise into my routine. At first it was really hard to push myself to do it, but with time it became so much easier. Research shows that through neuroplasticity the brain can learn a new habit in 21 days. Within three months, they can become even more hard-wired. Why does that matter? It means we don't have to think as much about doing them. It just becomes as natural as brushing your teeth. We start channelling our autopilot function into things that are useful.

This book is not just about introducing new habits but replacing old ones. Anxiety is a habit. Depression is a habit. Mental health disorders are where the brain has a habitual way of thinking that causes the body to react a certain way, helping contribute to the dysregulation of the nervous system. Therefore, if we introduce new habits, we can start to let go of the old ones. They may be habits that served us during childhood, but often, it's those that no longer serve us during adulthood.

Whilst sharing habits I have used, I also include some visualisation exercises. I will give an example of how powerful visualisation can be through a story my Great-Aunty told me. She is a retired English teacher, and she had a student who was completely engrossed in drawing the Pikachu character every lesson. He was not listening in class because he was so distracted. So as his teacher she had a word with him and asked him to hand her the Pikachu. She said she would look after him and hand him back at the end of every lesson. Every lesson thereon, the student gave his teacher an imaginary Pikachu character, and as a result, he would actually start listening in class. There was just one day where he had an issue later in the day and popped his head in class to remind his teacher that she hadn't given him Pikachu back! Visualisation is powerful. It is the practice of intentionally imagining something happening, as opposed to daydreaming, which is unintentional and unstructured. The reason visualisation is powerful is because studies prove that the subconscious does not know the difference between visualising something and actually seeing the real thing. The same part of the brain lights up in both scenarios.

I created an action plan to help implement habits that made huge changes in the way I lived, and still do. The action plan is towards the end of this book and includes hints & tips, as well as a 21-day schedule to help track progress of implementing these. Autopilot takes over after repeating a habit for 21 days, so the habit takes less effort. Autopilot can be our downfall, but it can also be a superpower if we choose for it to be! A routine is not 'one size fits all', and so it is merely suggestive rather than instructive. Ultimately, we as individuals are our own best guides, not anyone else.

Reflection question:

Can you identify habits of your own that you don't like?

For example, allowing your thoughts to spiral out of control and imagine the worst-case scenario. Notice when your thoughts are spiralling and revert your attention back to an anchor of the present moment, such as the breath. When it comes to changing habits, repetition is key. Therefore, keep reverting your attention as many times as necessary. It will get easier over time.

4. Is there another dimension to the mental health crisis?

I took my dog for a walk one evening. She was a springer spaniel called 'Fern' with a failing liver, and I knew that this would be the last walk I would take her on. My mum said she was not well enough to chase a ball, and so I didn't take one with me. We got to the sectioned-off area of the park where dogs are allowed off their lead. Fern looked at me with those expecting eyes, wondering where her ball was. I burst into tears. I was taking her on her final walk, and at this rate it was going to be a disappointing one. I regretted so much not bringing a ball, regardless of whether she was physically okay to fetch one. It was at this time I said to myself, "If there is a higher power out there, please now just give me a ball." Within 15 seconds of searching for one, I found one. I was so pleased, as was Fern! Of course, that could have all been coincidental and lucky, but I like to at least think 'what if.'

Having been raised in a Christian household, I had become resistant to religion in my adolescent years. This changed as I gradually brought my belief system into question—a process that is fundamental for creating a healthier mind. There are beliefs we have from childhood that can be damaging during adulthood. We might not even realise we have the belief itself. It can take some degree of self-analysis to recognise it. Coming back to spirituality, it was only when I opened my mind to the potential of there being a creator of the universe (God, Higher Power, whatever you want to call it) that I started to feel a gradual connection to something bigger. That something bigger showed up through timely opportunities that I perceived as more than just coincidence.

The power of faith I witnessed was most influential when I spent some time working on a strawberry farm in Western Australia. The farm had lots of immigrants from Vanuatu. They started their days listening to music. They got on with their strawberry picking and did the best they could despite not being rewarded any extra pay. They would finish the day cooking, chatting, and really laughing together. I happened to be there whilst they were celebrating the 42nd anniversary of independence from Britain too, and what became clearer was that they had a strong faith. That faith enabled them to believe all would be okay, which not only took the weight off of them individually, but brought them all together.

My psychosis diagnosis has left me more inquisitive of both hallucinations and the potential for these to be a spiritual experience. There is the theory that we all are experiencing an agreed hallucination, as it would be necessary as part of the evolutionary process for us to all see the same thing so that we can work together. Some may argue a spiritual experience is real, whereas a hallucination is not.

Having a wake-up call entails recognising the dissociation between the veneer you present to society and the actual reality beneath. I perceive a wake-up call to be the same as what society also refers to as a mid-life crisis. On average, most people experience one between the ages of 40 and 60 years old. Perhaps the age at which this happens will decrease in a world where everything external seems to be speeding up around us. The reason you may not be living authentically is because you are identified with thoughts. Often our thoughts run our lives. Living by the 'I should do this' because society says so. You are living a life based on who you think you should be rather than what might actually fulfil you. The wider the split between the surface of one's life and their inner reality, the greater the inauthenticity. The soul communicates its dissatisfaction through depression and anxiety. It wants to be listened to and heard.

I mentioned the soul because I think it's important to talk about. We improve mental well-being through more time spent engaging with our soul. Those who are less spiritual may just want to refer to it as the 'awareness' within them. To really explain what the soul is, it helps to compare behaviour of toddlers to adults. Toddlers are very present; they don't dwell on the past and future. They don't factor in other people's opinions. They get lost in having fun, and cry when their needs aren't met. They are not in a space of thought. They are in a state of observance. By this I mean being fully present. There is no thinking about the past or future. They are in touch with their senses. An interesting quote by Eckhart Tolle is, "I have lived with many Zen masters—all of them cats." Cats are a great example of being in the moment and therefore in a state of observance. Going back to the comparison of adult and child, clearly, there is a naivete in children that will naturally go away as they get older, as it should. However, we can choose to be more engaged with our soul, whilst also gaining wisdom through experience. Because if people are not in touch with their soul, they feel unfulfilled. It's as though there is a hole within them that they will try and fill by looking to the outside world. The means they may use to address this gap include food, TV, alcohol, cigarettes, drugs, lust, material possessions, body dysmorphia, money, workaholism, and power. They will constantly look to fill this hole, only achieving temporary pleasure or distraction from their emptiness, as opposed to long-term fulfilment.

I question whether there is a spiritual dimension to the mental health crisis. That is whether we have lost connection to our creator, and this is contributing to our suffering. I see a clear distinction between religion and Christianity for instance. In my view they are not the same thing. Religion is man's execution of Christianity. Christianity is having a healthy relationship with our creator (God, higher power). If we step back and look at the things that are happening in the world, you get the feeling that things weren't meant to be this way. It's for this reason that I question if there is a higher power that we may have lost connection to.

5. Self-reflect

"*Who looks outside dreams; who looks inside awakes*." -Carl Jung

A turning point for me where I started to delve into the world of mental health was the COVID-19 lockdown. I was able to work from home. My workload reduced. I had more time. I started to sleep better and eat better. I was given the chance to become more conscious of the fact that I had everything I wanted externally, yet I felt so numb. I rarely laughed or cried. I had no other choice but to really look at myself. This started with me questioning why I behaved the way I did in certain situations and realising that a common thread was acting based on my insecurities.

A powerful starting point is to self-reflect, but with an important consideration. That is, to look at all the parts we haven't liked about ourselves. Any regrets, upset and shame; all of the dark stuff. I find the following structure useful to self-reflect:

a) The first seven years

b) The conditioned self years (beyond seven)

A good starting point is to reflect upon the first seven years, because these years shape behaviours that play a large part in how we navigate our later lives. Our brain becomes wired by the behaviours that we repeat, and so whatever behaviours we have learnt by the age of seven, we are likely to continue repeating.

The first seven years

"Give me a child until he is seven, and I will show you the man." -Aristotle

It's our behaviours specifically with other people that heavily influence how we feel. We are humans, and one of our basic needs is to have connection with others. Attachment theory, developed by John Bowlby in the 1950s (Learning and Lang, 2020), says our relationships during childhood will determine what our attachment style is and therefore how we will behave in future relationships. There are four main attachment styles, which are the following:

a) Secure: A securely attached person can trust others and be trusted, love and accept love, and get close to others with relative ease.

b) Anxious: Tend to be very insecure about their relationships and so are hungry for validation.

c) Avoidant: Have trouble getting close to others or trusting others in relationships, and relationships can make them feel suffocated.

d) Fearful-Avoidant: Both desperately crave affection and want to avoid it at all costs.

UK statistics for % of people with an attachment style:

Type	*% of people as of 2022 in UK*
Secure	*55%*
Anxious	*8%*
Avoidant	*23%*
Fearful-avoidant	*14%*

These statistics suggest it's close to 50:50 as to whether you have a secure attachment style or a non-secure attachment style.

I grew up with parents who had their own mental health issues. My mum had what we thought was just depression, that would later be re-diagnosed as bipolar and ADHD. Meanwhile, my dad alternated between states of depression and anxiety. Together, they were using all their energies to meet my and my sister's practical needs. There gradually became less left to support our emotional needs. This showed up through them being withdrawn and exhausted. An inevitable consequence of my parent's poor well-being was a lack of space where I could easily express my emotions and feel off-loaded afterwards.

Not off-loading my emotions had consequences. I made a real effort to fit in with friends at school. There was a craving of validation. Note the crossover of this with the description of an anxious attachment recently. There was a particular incident where this need to fit in was threatened. It was break-time at school. A bigger boy came up and started hitting me. It came as a shock, and

I was very confused as to why he was doing it. It turned out he thought I had stolen his hat and scarf, and he was punishing me for it. Then the teacher intervened and asked me to return the hat and scarf to the student.

Later that afternoon, the teacher called me into the middle of class during a circle time. She started shouting at me and ragging at my school shirt.

“Rachel, you needed to have returned Johnny's hat and scarf. How would you like it if I stole your shirt from you?"

I was so startled that I couldn't say anything. My heart was racing, but my body had frozen.

When my dad picked me up, he noticed I wasn't wearing the hat and scarf.

"Where is your hat and scarf?" Dad said.

“The teacher took them off of me.”

My dad dragged me back to the classroom.

“Can I have my daughter’s hat and scarf back please?”

Mrs Lovatt didn’t apologise.

“She should’ve said her name was on them.”

She didn't understand that I was terrified and unable to say anything. There are many dimensions to this story and my response to the events that are framed by my childhood and my attachment style.

First off, there was an inability to speak up for myself. When stressed, it is neurologically proven that the area of the brain that is able to think logically, being the prefrontal cortex, shuts down. This is why, after we have those heated arguments, we come up with things we wish we said later on. Our prefrontal cortex starts activating itself once we have relaxed again. The reason it shut down to begin with was to enable the release of stress hormones that prepare the body to fight the threat or flee from the danger. A state of panic was induced, and so I was not capable of defending myself. I'd say this is a fairly normal reaction, irrespective of someone's attachment style.

Secondly, why was the state of fight-and-flight I was in so debilitating, given that I wasn't facing anything life-threatening? Due to my already established insecurities, I was experiencing an extra level of stress associated with being the centre of attention for all the wrong reasons. The need to fit in with others as a form of validation was being threatened. There was an unresolved emotion being triggered that heightened my stress response. This unresolved emotion would get projected onto relationships with others, particularly my sister.

At the end of every lunchtime at school, my sister would come and kiss to say good-bye until the end of the day. This continued until I noticed that a teacher had seen us in the distance and expressed delight in her face at how sweet this interaction was. I saw this reaction, and it led to me cutting off that interaction with my sister. I always thought this was because the teacher's attention made me feel exposed, and I was potentially doing something outside of social norms. It would have been a dysfunctional reaction, but it was aligned with my existing coping mechanisms of trying to blend in with others. Writing this now, however, I have realised the extra dimension to this story and why it's useful to reflect on our past and see things from a different perspective.

Although the issue may have partly been that I feared I was not fitting in with my peers, in hindsight, it was more that I found seeing this teacher smiling very triggering. I didn't know it at the time, but it was because she was the same teacher that embarrassed me regarding the hat and scarf incident. This woman had shown no accountability and not apologised to me for the mistakes made that day. She hadn't told off the boy for hitting me, she hadn't given me the opportunity to have my say, and she had shown me up in front of a class, physically tugging at my shirt and shouting. This was why I stopped having what was a sweet interaction with my sister. I didn't want to see this teacher happy. It was resentment being projected in the form of retaliation, without any of my thinking behind it. There was no consciousness. It was my unconscious. The majority of the decisions we make are said to rely on the 95 percent of brain activity that is unconscious (The Oklahoman, n.d.).

There is a final dimension to the incident with the boy and teacher, which is subjective. I have questioned why I wasn't trusted on multiple occasions. The boy didn't trust that I hadn't stolen his hat and scarf. The teacher automatically assumed I'd stolen them. I believe I hadn't gained people's trust because I wasn't being authentic. I was suppressing my true self by trying to conform to my friend's behaviour so extensively, and I think those that are being more authentic pick up on it. For me it may have shown up through a lack of eye contact, reservedness, and extreme self-control in an attempt to avoid facing negative emotions.

When I met new people during this time in my life, I often would presume they didn't like me. I now realise there is a science to this behaviour. There is such a thing as perceiving neutral facial expressions as threats (Yoon and Zinbarg, 2008). If we met new people when we were cavemen and couldn't read their facial expressions, we wouldn't trust them, and so they wouldn't be accepted into the tribe. But such a presumption only needs to be made when in a stressful situation. A new person approaching you in cavemen days would've been stressful, as they could've easily wanted to steal from you or worse. But in day-to-day life, I find this presumption one worth letting go of.

At this stage I was a fearful-avoidant attachment style, what is also referred to as a disorganised attachment style. At school I showed a fearful or anxious tendency where I intensely wanted validation from others, but never directly asked for it. This is one of the reasons the incident with the teacher was quite so triggering. It subconsciously felt like a threat to gaining validation from others. For me a form of validation from others was fitting in with them and therefore feeling accepted, but this incident involved showing me up, and so I instead stuck out like a sore thumb. Conversely at home, the avoidant side came out, where I became more withdrawn. The reason I share my reflection here is to show that from reflecting on what seemed small events in my childhood, I began to connect dots that would create a bigger picture. The bigger picture was that there was unresolved emotion at the root of all my toxic behaviours that needed addressing. I'd start to share segments of this process with family, who would be surprised because I seemed okay. Seeming okay should not be relied upon as an indicator of a secure attachment style. When we don't have a secure attachment style, our body will develop coping mechanisms. It’s these coping mechanisms that will make us appear okay. However, for as long as there is a coping mechanism in place, there is a dissociation between a person and their feelings. This dissociation will grow wider until the person wakes up.

Reflection question

What attachment style would you say you are? There are attachment style quizzes accessible online.

If you don't have a secure attachment, do not worry. The chapters within this book are designed to help you have a more secure attachment style through becoming more in tune with yourself.

Becoming aware of the conditioned self

"Watch your thoughts; they become words.
Watch your words; they become actions.
Watch your actions; they become habits.
Watch your habits; they become character.
Watch your character; it becomes your destiny." - Lao-Tze

That person we are conditioned to become at the age of seven is not necessarily aligned with who we want to be, and the wider that gap is, the greater the suffering will be. On the surface, I was successful. My family would say how mature and independent I was throughout my childhood and adolescent years. I was in consistent employment from the age of 13. I had lots of friends. I got straight A's in my exams. I was accepted onto a five-year apprenticeship to train as a chartered accountant with a big-four firm, whilst also completing a sponsored degree. By 20 I had all of this in place, and I'd bought a house with my boyfriend. However, no matter how good the external circumstances may have seemed, I still had wired within me a fearful-avoidant attachment style. There was a different reality beneath the surface-level success. I had become mature and independent because I didn't know how to open up and show vulnerability. That also meant that despite being physically present with friends and family, mentally, I was becoming more and more dissociated.

I too felt dissociated at work. I've reflected on why I chose accounting as a career. There were two key reasons. The first was that I always wanted to be prepared for worst-case scenarios, and that meant being financially comfortable. Becoming a chartered accountant would offer a secure and steady income. The second reason I chose it as a career was because I did well in Maths at school, and so it seemed the next logical step. The truth of the matter was that I was not naturally good at Maths at school. I had to try extra hard relative to the average student in my class. The reason I had incentive to try extra hard was because I liked the comfort of knowing if an answer was right or wrong. It didn't matter if I was wrong, as long as I knew. I hated the grey area of uncertainty, which you didn't find in Maths.

If anyone was to ask if I was okay, the answer would always be yes. I became an actress, with the façade of a successful, happy person. The reality was I had emotional baggage that was building up and up. I was not confronting any of these emotions. They would either leak through anxiety attacks or get projected in the form of holding grudges against people. Yet I had no awareness that there was a root cause of these negative emotions that I needed to face. I just pushed through because I had such tunnel vision on passing my exams. I would find some relief through a never-ending want list. But once I earned better money and realised buying things did not fix my problems, I could only find an outlet in television, mostly crime documentaries. I don't believe it to be a coincidence that the True Crime genre is booming at the same time as a mental health crisis. It has become a source of distraction and comfort for many whilst trying to make it through the day. I think the genre can appeal to people who have mental health issues because subconsciously it reminds us that there are people out there with far bigger struggles.

In summary, I have an insecure attachment style, developed in childhood to protect me, which is now causing harm. We know that the mind is shaped in the first seven years of our lives, and it is the mind that is now running our behaviours. My mind has power over me by over-planning future events, over-dwelling on past events, attempting to mind-read others, holding grudges, and so on.

Once you become aware of your own cycle of consistent thoughts, there is an opportunity to make change. You have become aware of your thoughts and therefore realise that you are not your thoughts. Once you realise this, and for me it took time, there is a great opportunity to improve mental well-being. Each time you are aware of your thoughts, you're engaging with your true self.

Reflection question

When did you last reflect on your upbringing? Are you able to identify coping mechanisms you developed that served you during your school years? If yes, do you still want these coping mechanisms during adulthood? If not, you have the power to change these wired behaviours; identification is the hardest part.

6. Want what you have

"A happy person builds their inner world, while an unhappy person blames the outside world." -T. Harv Eker

When I let myself imagine what will make me happy, I picture having a big house in the countryside, with two beautiful horses and the freedom to travel the world as and when I wish. Perhaps there is something you have in mind that you believe will make you happy. If you visualise it and sit with whatever feeling it creates in you for as long and intensely as you can, slowly, the feeling will pass. With that, we can teach ourselves that we cannot rely on a change in external circumstance to give us happiness, for if the event itself was to actually happen, we know the rewarding feelings would still pass. Emotions are just sensations in the body, and they will fluctuate no matter how much we improve our external circumstances. If there is anything that observing fame has taught us, it's that someone can afford everything and still feel life is not worth living.

The mind is a problem-solver. Therefore, if we don't feel okay, the mind will try and resolve it. The issue is that the mind will only focus on things in the outside world. There are two reasons this is the case. The first is that the outside material world is all that we can see. The second is because that was what was necessary when we were cavemen. Feeling bad is part of our threat system that acts as a warning, and when we were cavemen, it was much more accurate (Mi-Psych | Mindfulness & Clinical Psychology Solutions, 2017). However, the modern world has escalated far quicker than our bodies have. When identified with our thoughts, we might say, 'if I just had this, I would be happy.' Once we say 'I'll be happy when', we are in effect delaying happiness. Of course, I can only speak from the experience of myself and being brought up with a roof over my head, a family structure, and living in a developed part of the world. I was raised in fortunate circumstances.

Since a large contribution to suffering is the result of a gap between what we have, and what we want, I decided to change my approach. I wanted to work on my mind and close this gap. I started to list three things I was grateful for each day. Research shows that gratitude can lead to a multitude of health improvements, including better sleep and lower stress. What I found was at the beginning, it was really hard to come up with three things. I worked through this by looking at what I was surrounded with and then pictured these things disappearing.

Whether it was my favourite spot in the office to sit in or the warm feeling someone in the room gave me. Then within a few weeks, I was coming up with things throughout the whole day that I was grateful for. It really lifted not just my mood but people around me. When I picked the rarer things, it required more thinking, which helped to strengthen this new mindset. I was looking at things that had always seemed so trivial, such as running water, and not just saying I appreciated it, but really feeling gratitude for it.

It would be a few months until I realised I was feeling much more joyful. My numbness was starting to shift into gratitude. This reflected the diversion of my attention away from negative thoughts to more of what was going well. Having a mindset of focusing on the positives did not mean turning a blind eye to the negatives. Bad things would still happen, but I was much less fazed by them. I would find myself seeking positives from bad things. For instance, if I was stuck in traffic, I'd be grateful for access to the radio. Alternatively, if I couldn't see any good in it, I would have faith that it was there to teach me something.

Scientists have found that those who take note of their gratitude are likely to have higher self-esteem, feel happier, and even improved immune system health (Brown and Wong, 2017). This makes sense since we know stress hormones weaken the immune system.

Statistics also show that simply journaling for five minutes a day about what we are grateful for can enhance our long-term happiness by over 10 percent.

Gratitude is about becoming conscious that we all have our own individual perception of reality based on the narrative that plays in our head, and that we have power over what that narrative says. Ultimately, that narrative has power over how we feel. Life is about the little things. It becomes much more fulfilling when we seek these out rather than live in apprehension for 'bigger' things to come. This is not to say that in the present moment we will always be happy. It's about accepting the present moment and heightening observance to acknowledge where there are still blessings.

Exercise

List three things you are grateful for right now. How do they make you feel? (Don't worry if you don't feel a lot the first time. It took me weeks to start noticing a difference.)

7. Being present through mindfulness

"I've had a lot of worries in my life, most of which never happened." -Mark Twain

I realised I was living in a vicious cycle when I started to lose control over how much sugary food I was craving. It started to become such a normal thing to order in fast food to round off a long, tiring day. What was worse was that it was normal for me to start off my day feeling tired. I wasn't getting good-quality sleep. It was not unusual for me to make silly mistakes at work, which I largely put down to this unhealthy lifestyle. It is this and other vicious cycles that often go hand in hand with depression and anxiety.

The vicious cycle:

The mundane job to earn money
The attention economy (Netflix, social media, etc.)
High-sugar food
Zero exercise
Poor sleep

I was deeply in this cycle. I believe that it's up to individuals to break it. In doing so, they will see dramatic impacts on their mental health. Those chemical imbalances in the brain that are seen amongst people with mental illness are likely to become balanced as addressing this vicious cycle will help to regulate the nervous system. I think that the worst place to try and start the change is sleep. As soon as you put pressure on yourself to get a good night's sleep, the opposite happens. Instead, it is better to focus on the small things you can control, such as reducing the amount of bread consumed (or any other sugary foods). I personally found reducing sugar intake really affected the quality of my sleep and therefore my state of mind. I decided to reduce my sugar intake because I knew that the amount of chocolate I was going through in the evenings was coming from a place of greed, and it was making me feel guilty and rubbish. This change of behaviour influenced my sleep so that I fell asleep faster. My sleep also seemed deeper, since I felt more refreshed the following morning. Similarly, reducing the binge-watching of a series from two episodes to one episode an evening made a significant difference. The vicious cycle is a coping mechanism for being on never-ending autopilot. There is no consciousness. Where there is no consciousness, there is no fulfilment because you're just living like a robot. When I chose to access consciousness through mindfulness meditation, it started to have a positive domino effect on the vicious cycle.

Meditation enables us to rewire the brain so that we live more fully in the present moment. If we attempt a routine of mindfulness meditation even five minutes a day, the mindfulness practised then filters through the remainder of the day. Imagine you're an alien that's just stepped into your body and the human experience is new to you. This experience of novelty and the awareness it engenders is an example of mindfulness. When done consistently, it feels liberating, as the mind quietens.

I personally completed a mindfulness course offered in CD and book format by Mark Williams, an Oxford professor (Williams and Penman, 2011). Within two weeks, I was noticing changes. I first noticed it was making a difference when I was doing the dishes, and I realised I wasn't thinking. I was present. This was foreign territory. There was significant change within myself on days where I'd started with mindfulness, as opposed to the ones where I'd immediately start thinking about all the things I had to do for the day. It made me come to realise that my problems were created in my own head.

Because I was wasting less energy on consistent thinking, I started to become conscious of things in my life that needed changing. In particular, I became conscious of the vicious cycle I was living in, and I wanted to change it. It started small with small steps, including not doing any overtime at work. Previously, I had always felt selfish for drawing boundaries around my workday. Then I realised by putting up these boundaries and prioritising myself, I was actually able to have more energy in the long run. I started to perform much better. A big part of my performance improvement was because I was now able to step back and see the bigger picture when doing work that required deeper thinking. I always struggled with seeing the bigger picture before, which is a symptom of being in a recurrent fear state; we have tunnel vision. This is when we can seem to lack common sense.

The brain is so tunnel-visioned it won't connect dots that seem so obvious from the perspective of someone who is not in a survival mode. My concentration significantly improved. I was no longer living life by the clock and instead just accepted I could only do one thing at a time and that the one thing I completed I knew would be of better quality if I did it from a place of calm. My focus then started to shift onto bigger problems that I'd previously never had the awareness to address. It resulted in the ending of a long-term relationship, a career break, and the beginning of travelling.

The intention of mindfulness meditation is not to quiet the thoughts, but to practise connecting with the awareness of the thoughts. All that matters is repeated practice. All of this is not to say I don't still have days where I can get caught up in 'the vicious cycle'. However now, when I do, I'm at least conscious of it. I know the exact cause of why I'm in it and have a plan to come out of it. Researchers reviewed more than 200 studies of mindfulness among healthy people and found mindfulness-based therapy was especially effective for reducing stress, anxiety, and depression (Apa.org, 2021).

It was also through mindfulness meditation that I came to realise what the mind-body connection meant. One of the practices that most clarified this connection was the body scan. As I'd go to sleep and get relaxed, I'd focus on the most intense areas of tension and really feel them. A memory would show up, for which I was then able to access the associated emotion. I would feel the tension ease the more intensely I felt this emotion.

Those that know they have an overactive mind but are not aware of any physical tensions may actually just have a very weak mind-body connection. This was me. I'd spent 20 years gradually hiding from my emotions, so I actually didn't know what I was feeling. I was always seeking distractions from what I thought was numbness. That numbness was a huge wall between my mind and body. When I'd eventually acknowledge the numbness, there would be deep emotions and tensions that would come to light. Many of us work in full-time jobs that only require the use of our mind. If we don't put in practices to check in with our feelings or do mindful physical activity, we risk being dissociated from our real feelings. This is how many go on to have a mid-life crisis. If feelings don't get acknowledged, they don't go away. They build up, and they can cause people to break down, which is the body's attempt of shouting to the mind, 'Please listen to me!'

Reflection question

Over the next day, start paying attention to where your thoughts are. How often are you thinking compared to being present, i.e., in a state of observance where there is no thought? Should you want to reduce how much you think, consider incorporating mindfulness meditation into your routine.

8. Accept help

At the time of writing this book, I have been admitted to psychiatric wards. It made me question everything I was sharing within this book because I thought I was moving backwards. As time has moved on, I am now grateful for those ward admissions. I had just gotten stuck on my journey and reached a place where I needed the extra help. In actuality, it was help that would enable me to move further forward in my mental health journey.

It is estimated that 75 percent of people with mental health problems in England may not get access to the treatment they need (Mental Health Foundation, 2022). There's a whole host of reasons why this may be, whether there still is the stigma attached to asking for help, or insufficient government funding for these services. It is perhaps why the self-help book industry is booming in recent years. In the UK in 2019, we saw a record level of 3 million sales, a 20 percent increase from the previous year (Walker, 2019). I see this book as an offering in the self-help genre. However, I in no way wish to refute the importance of being able to ask for and accept external help. This is from my own personal experience.

Without support from nurses and doctors, I would not be better now. Being better today means the nurses found an optimum level of medication for me, and I am practising healthy habits. The medication enables me to fit back into society and live a normal life, something I previously took for granted. There were lots of things I learnt on the ward. Having lived quite isolated before, I wasn't as aware of the extent to which everyone really does have their own problems. Sometimes, it can feel like it's just you. You are not alone. We all have our own struggles, and this is the nature of life. The way we respond to these struggles determines the course that we take, and there is no shame in asking for help. Even if it's talking to someone on a helpline—it's what they're there for!

My headspace was completely emotional. There was no reasoning, which meant I was jumping to conclusions, being presumptuous of other people, and not considering alternative explanations. I was creating my own reality that was far from the truth. The underlying belief in this false reality was that 'everything is my fault'. As I progress post-discharge from the ward, I start to find some rationale for events that happened, and it's when we have a balance between emotion and reason that we can live with a wiser mindset. A place of greater peace and logic.

My time on the ward showed me first-hand how differently we behave when we're in survival mode as opposed to a safe and secure environment. It is up to us to either change our environments to make them safe and secure, or, if that's not doable, then teach the brain that the existing environment is safe and secure. We do this by changing our thoughts.

Reflection question

Do you feel you could ask for professional help if having a mental health crisis? If not, please challenge this and discuss with other people, rather than leave it as a fixed viewpoint, which could be a risky stance in the long run since *everyone* has to take care of their mental health.

9. Choose your values

It's all well saying that you're going to be more authentic, but does the authentic person have a positive influence on others? They might not. It might instead be the case that beneath the façade and people-pleasing, there is a hurt person who needs healing. This is why I see it as a necessity to know what our values are, so we have at least something to guide the decisions we make. I define my own values as the following: integrity, empathy, courage and faith (a trust that things will be okay).

There are a number of approaches to identifying your values:

1. Ask close friends and family what they perceive your main values to be.

2. List what you perceive your main values to be, using recurrent behaviours to support them.

3. List what you wish your main values were and reflect on whether you think you act in line with these values. Alternatively, what changes would need to be made for you to act in line with these values?

How do people who know their values live their lives differently? There is research to show how our values guide us. Lior Abramson and her colleagues ran a study in Israel to find an answer to this question. The study involved 243 children between 5 and 12 years old. The children first completed the values picture questionnaire. From their answers, the scientists computed a score for their prosocial values. Prosocial values are about being kind, helpful, and supportive of others. If a child had a high score, the scientists knew that prosocial values were very important to this child. The higher the children's scores of prosocial values, the more they shared in situations. This means that our values guide our behaviour in situations that come with some costs to ourselves. When there are no costs, most people will happily share—it is easy. But when we have to make difficult decisions, that's when values matter (Döring and Knafo-Noam, 2019).

For me, choosing my values by no means has made me into a 'perfectly behaved' person. What it does is guide my decisions. I believe that those who have a stronger moral compass are more likely to be kinder and confident people. What we may consider our core values may change over time depending on external circumstances.

Something I struggled with was beneath the façade. I found a part of myself that was actually fearful, distrusting, and sceptical. Some may identify this part as the inner child. Of course, that is not who I want to be. While it's okay to say that you're going to be more authentic, who is the authentic person? I believe we have to see the authentic person to know what needs changing. For me, I had to learn to trust not just people, but the process of life. I also had to stop trying to control every little thing. As I made these decisions and prioritised basic necessities like sleep and food, I became a more relaxed and joyful person again, but this time it was genuine rather than forced. I now choose to trust people until they give me a reason not to trust. It's far easier living life this way than being sceptical of every person you come across.

Reflection question

Do you know what your values are? They can be based on what you consider to be most important in your life and perhaps what already comes more naturally. That way, it will be easier to notice should you start acting out of line. Listed on the next page are some suggestions:

Loyalty	Courage
Spirituality	Tolerance
Humility	Trustworthiness
Compassion	Equanimity
Honesty	Altruism
Kindness	Appreciation
Integrity	Empathy
Selflessness	Toughness
Determination	Self-Reliance
Generosity	Attentiveness

10. Re-parent yourself

"Perfection is the biggest obstacle to striving for excellence." – Brené Brown

I remember my grandma saying that, when faced with a problem, she could still imagine what her late father would say about how to deal with it. When she said it, I realised I didn't have access to an inner dialogue where I felt supported or guided. In the UK, approximately 68 percent of women and 57 percent of men with mental health problems are parents (www.mentalhealth.org.uk, n.d.). These rates could be even higher depending on how open men and women are about their issues. Given how many parents have their own issues, I believe it can only benefit their children to learn to re-parent themselves as adults. This means to develop a relationship with their inner child. The inner child is the part of us that holds on to insecurities developed as part of belief systems inherited and shaped during the first seven years. The concept of the inner child was first proposed by psychologist Carl Jung after he examined his own childlike inner-feelings and emotions. We have the power to tell that child within us which beliefs we want to let go of, and to exchange them for new ones.

By no means does re-parenting yourself mean that your parents did a bad job. The nature of being human is that we're imperfect. We wouldn't be here without imperfection. We make mistakes. We don't suddenly overcome this when we become parents. We'll still make mistakes. Many grow up exposed to living patterns that don't serve them. Often people blame their parents for it. A part of the healing process I believe is necessary is seeing how our parents did the best they could with the level of awareness they had.

Because we don't live with extended families and spend most of our time growing up with parents, we have less opportunity to have a wider perspective on what behaviours are toxic. Toxicity becomes our normality. Examples of toxicity amongst families can be more obvious, such as shouting and arguing non-constructively, but there are less obvious examples. For instance, being very nice and polite to one another. If done alongside a lack of openness, it can cause a child to subconsciously feel that they don't want to express negative emotions because it will disrupt the 'nice' atmosphere. It can be very difficult for people to become aware of these behaviours and step outside of them.

To re-parent yourself means to acknowledge negative patterns and choose to change them. You also learn to trust yourself, which for me meant becoming a more confident person in general. For example, I was given a new job role at my workplace whilst travelling. All my anxiety kicked in because I would be the only one doing that role, and so everyone would be dependent on me. I was overwhelmed, and because I was in that state, I did a bad job of it too. Rather than try and force myself through it and prove to myself I could do it, I instead questioned whether it was worth the energy. I knew I was capable of it if I really put my mind to it, but I decided it wasn't worth it. That same day, I told my manager I wanted to step down to my previous role. I was so relieved and grateful to myself for not forcing myself to do something I didn't want to do. I developed a self-trust where I was now capable of choosing my challenges, and this was not one worth bothering with.

A big part of re-parenting yourself is to put up boundaries. It can require following less of the mind's 'shoulds', and more of the intuition. In particular it is useful in those instances where we get FOMO—'fear of missing out'. Rather than go out because of FOMO, FOMO is a great opportunity to sit with that uncomfortable emotion. When we participate in things with reluctance, we're neglecting ourselves. That reluctance is there for a reason. Having time to ourselves to do nothing can be stigmatised because it can be perceived as being 'lazy.' I'd argue the very opposite. It requires effort and discipline to set out time to be truly with yourself. Humans need self-connection.

The more I have put up boundaries and said no to things, not only have I felt less guilt and regret, but it's turned into an energy that I have had more choice in directing. It means I now have more genuine energy for the social events I say yes to.

Whatever lifts your mood, and your inner child's mood, is really worth incorporating into your days. However, being human can mean we're less likely to prioritise things that are not necessities. There's no point fighting against this resistance since it's wasted energy and defeats the purpose of play. But we can try and work with it by simplifying the play activities. Just something little is better than nothing. The two activities I find most effective when I really don't fancy doing anything are the following:

- Playing some music. This has been shown to have a number of health benefits including to relieve stress and improve concentration.

- Shaking my body. This can help to relieve tensions caused by stress or trauma. It helps to calm the body. 30 seconds can be all you need.

During the re-parenting process, I have patience with myself, which means not being self-critical or frustrated when I don't stick to a routine I've set myself. To actually be great at all forms of self-care is impossible, because that would be adhering to perfection, something that does not exist.

Reflection question

Do you have a relationship with your inner child? It would be most notable in stressful situations where you have access to an inner voice that tells you everything will be okay. If not, then consider trying to access it.

____

____

____

____

____

____

____

____

____

____

____

Here are some suggestions on how to facilitate this:

- When did you last have self-critical thoughts? What did they say? For instance, what was your inner narrative when you last made a mistake? It can be useful to think of the self critic as the inner child. The inner child might say, 'I'm so stupid.' It's then up to you to challenge that. You might respond 'No, you're not. You're trying and learning, and that's all that matters.'

- When did you last feel upset? How would you speak to your own friend or child to make them feel better? Try and apply that narrative to yourself.

11. Let go of grudges

"To forgive is to set a prisoner free and discover that the prisoner was you." - Lewis B. Smedes

I felt reluctant to forgive my teacher who accused me of stealing another student's hat and scarf, as I discussed earlier. I did not want to forgive her for humiliating me because I did not want to condone her actions. I eventually realised forgiveness is not condonement. It is possible to forgive someone and still entirely disagree with their actions. It does not mean that the other person has gotten away with it. It is not your responsibility to punish them via a grudge. In fact, the only person we harm by holding a grudge is ourselves. Holding grudges is a burden. It's for that reason we need to choose to forgive if we want to improve our mental well-being. Studies have found that the act of forgiveness can lower the risk of heart attack and improve cholesterol levels and sleep, as well as reducing levels of anxiety, depression, and stress (Toussiant, Shields and Slavich, 2016).

It was only once I started to become more present that I became aware of just how much I needed to forgive in order to let go of the past. My dreams were arguments with school friends. I could never really remember what we were arguing about, but I'd wake up left with the feeling that it was real. There were a lot of people I had to forgive, including people no longer in my life. The person who I had to forgive most for was myself. I harboured regrets and a lot of guilt over my actions and inaction. Rather than resist these emotions, I embraced them. I tried to learn from them. In particular, I learnt that guilt is our body indicating that we have gone against our values. That was ironically relieving as I realised I did have values, but I'd just not been listening and acting on them. I realised deep down I must be a good person. I was owning my past, in an attempt to become more in tune with this good person.

Knowing that there is a difference between a person's conditioned self and their true self became my greatest asset for letting go of the past. I believe dysfunctional actions will always be sourced from the conditioned self. The true self is in touch with the moral compass. A moral compass is something I believe we all have within us. Being human means trying to manage these two conflicting sides of ourselves. We all have light and dark within us.

Therefore, we have to question what insecurity or trauma has led to a person's dysfunctional decisions. And who are we to judge if we've not taken into account that person's life?

Robert Maxwell was a British media figurehead but turned out to be a fraud and a corrupt person. There is a scene in a documentary where he is being filmed back at his hometown in Czechoslovakia, and he is standing at the foot of a huge gravestone (www.bbc.co.uk, n.d.). It turns out his whole family was wiped out during the Nazi Occupation. It is clear in this scene that his whole life, he had been running away from the pain that this caused. This analysis does not excuse his actions at all. But it does show the complete disconnect from his moral compass stemmed from pain.

For me, the forgiveness I was able to offer others was limited by the extent of forgiveness I was able to give to myself. The more I forgave myself, the easier it became to let go of grudges towards others.

The following steps were involved in the process of forgiveness.

A six-step process for forgiving others:

1 Pick one memory associated with the person you're angry or upset with. Note: don't disregard the things that seem 'very little', as they will often lead you to deeper issues beneath.

2 Set an intention of wanting to forgive this person. Although the intention is to forgive the person, it matters less whether you actually forgive that person, and more that the triggered emotions are actually processed. It is these emotions that will be burdening you.

3 Really feel the anger, rage, hurt, guilt, etc. Feel every emotion associated with this memory, without storytelling and being in the mind. Just let the emotions peak within you. Keep your attention at a present-moment anchor, such as the breath, to avoid being distracted by the mind. Sit with what arises for as long as you need to. Emotions are just sensations in the body, and eventually, they lose their impact, whilst you hold them in focus.

4 Once you've calmed down, put some pen to paper and write as though you're chatting to a counsellor. This gets better with practice and can become very useful when you learn how to create this relationship with yourself. What would you want a counsellor to ask you? If you cannot think of anything, then just propose the question 'how does that make you feel?' and keep following up with 'Why?' The idea is that you're able to express the hurt and reach some clarity.

5 Answer the following questions:

a) What do you think has led this person to behave this way? Considering that it is likely a pattern developed during childhood.

b) What can I learn from this?

6 Forgiving a person means there is no negative feeling triggered within you when thinking back on them or the event. Acknowledge if ever you reach this point. It's okay if you don't.

When we shed our pasts, we actually start to permit ourselves to be more authentic.

12. Listen to your intuition

Anxiety is a guide. I've learnt many lessons from it by seeing at what points in my life it was most intense. A key thing I noticed is it showed up when I wasn't being myself. For example, my anxiety heightened during my years of being a waitress. There are some people naturally suited to hospitality, and I was not one of them. I felt as though I couldn't always be myself, as this self would not be high-energy or welcoming enough for a customer. I had to try and imitate the behaviours of my peers. I was suppressing something that wanted to be expressed for most of my life as I tried to blend in. Eventually, I would change my approach and pay attention to my gut, which guided me towards decisions that allowed me to be myself. If I struggled to trust what my gut was saying, I'd find it useful to imagine what I wanted somebody to tell me who I really trusted. If ever I reverted to comparing myself to others, I recognised that was further ratcheting up energies within me. If I just redirected this energy to making actual changes for myself, I was giving it authentic expression. Anxiety doesn't have to be expressed through dramatic life changes. I started small with creativity, learning, exercising my mind-body connection through meditation, and stretching. There are a range of channels that can be unique to an individual.

Too many of us neglect, or perhaps are not even in tune with, our intuition. The demands of the labour force have gradually become more analytical and mind-focused, to cater to the advancement in technologies. We have excelled at using this part of our body because we're in a habit of using this part. We are less in the habit of using our intuition. How often do we want to do one thing and then let the mind convince us to do another thing? I believe the mind and intuition can be in sync, but it requires an initial step of really listening to the intuition and acting on it.

The more disconnected someone becomes from their intuition, the bigger the actions they may have to take to become aligned with it. I had to do it myself. I'd spent over five years training to be a chartered accountant. I passed the final big exam on the second attempt. It took all of my efforts, and I was burnt out. If I'd listened to the mind, it would say that I need to see through my career to make the exam successes worthwhile. But my intuition did not like that prospect. It wouldn't be until I picked up a bookmark one evening that had been sitting idle on my coffee table that I was able to make a decision. As I was getting ready to throw it out, I noticed an animation on it. It was a picture of a girl sitting with her head in her palm, staring out of the window, with a pile of self-help books next to her. I thought, 'That is going to be me.' I was doing all this inner work, but I was making no big decisions. I handed in my notice and started travelling. It was only with hindsight that I could reflect, and my mind could make logic out of it and align with my intuition. From being in a new environment, I was able to see all the transferable skills I had gained from my career thus far that I could apply anywhere else, but with much greater energy, and so could make me much more useful.

I was so happy that I'd listened to my gut. I had no concerns because I knew it felt right. Things were going my way. There was an ease about things and little coincidences where I just felt so fortunate. I had never had that feeling before, and I didn't want to lose it. To keep in touch with it, I began a journaling habit, to build on a trusting relationship with myself.

This was how I became my own therapist. Perhaps we could all access this inner therapist if we practised writing on a page and seeing what comes out.

In a 2006 study, almost 100 young adults spent 15 minutes journaling, drawing about a stressful event, or writing about their plans for the day, twice during one week (Newman, 2020). The people who journaled saw the biggest reduction in symptoms like depression, anxiety, and hostility. This was true even though 80 percent had rarely journaled about their feelings before. I appreciate that some people don't like writing. I do, but I also love talking. I often talk to myself out loud when I'm by myself. There was a time in my life where I was so withdrawn that I didn't even talk to myself anymore. I hadn't realised the true value of it.

Therefore, if you're not interested in the following journaling exercise, consider having an outright conversation with yourself instead.

Journaling exercise

I think there are a multitude of avenues that can be taken with journaling. For me, these were the following:

1) To work through unresolved emotions with an eye to acceptance. If unsure how to access unresolved emotions or where to start, I found the most recent time I got triggered as a good starting point. Leaning into the emotions and having a cry or feeling angry in your own private and safe space is very therapeutic. A useful technique is to say how something makes you feel and to keep asking why. You know you've reached an end point when you reach a positive emotion or relief.

2) A brain dump. I'd write down all of my trivial worries and get them off my chest that day. They say when you have a song stuck in your head, you should listen to it all the way through because your mind just wants to complete the loop of it. Similar to worrisome thoughts, the mind has a better time letting go of them when we work through them until we reach an absolute worst-case scenario and sit with it.

Recognising that no amount of worry can prepare us for something is an opportunity to sit with unresolved emotion behind the worry. It also helps to distinguish what's within your control and what isn't. Once you've identified something as not being within your control, it's easier to accept the uncertainty it provokes within you. An unexpected benefit for me was that I could visualise myself handing over that baggage to my inner parent ready to face the next morning—when I had scheduled journaling time. I could then be much more present in the meantime.

3) To set intentions for the day. This enabled me to spend the day focusing on one thing at a time, rather than worrying about all the things I had to do. We can utilise intentions that we have established to guide us toward which task we will do on completion of a previous one, therefore remaining present.

I limit my time to plan and reflect so that it is sourced from a place of presence rather than taking me away from being present. Journaling has been the most effective means for me to maintain my self-connection and to allow the direction I move in be guided by it rather than by comparing myself to others.

13. Learn to surrender

Once I started to make efforts to be more in touch with my intuition, I began to enter a transitional period in my life. During this period, I discovered the need to surrender. That meant just accepting what was. Physically, I would find often my body was not accepting of what was. It showed up in feelings of tension, clenched teeth, and generally being on edge. Oftentimes, the tension would gather in my legs and shoulders. I knew this was due to me not being accepting of what was; there was a clear change in my body language when things went my way as opposed to when things didn't go my way. I would check in with myself during the day and always find somewhere I needed to make an effort to relax. While it requires a greater level of self-awareness, the body can eventually learn to relax itself.

It's most important to check in with yourself when waking up in the morning and before going to sleep at night. Just ask, 'How am I feeling?' It gives you power. I found the worst thing was to wake up and start scrolling on my phone. It would only take one post to make me feel something negative, and I would carry that through my day. Whereas if we spend time with ourselves and check in, we have more power over the course of our day, as our mood can really set the tone and influence the outcome.

This is why it's good to have at least one practice first thing in the morning, even if it's just making the bed. It can be used as a measure. It means on the days you're not making your bed, or you're not making yourself breakfast, your mental health may be declining.

Struggling to surrender is also what causes us discomfort in the inevitable chores in life such as doing the dishes, waiting in a shop queue, or being stuck behind a slow car. Underneath all these behaviours is actually a sense of anxiety, and if we could just practise observing that feeling rather than resisting it in the form of road rage or impatience, these little nuances could become big opportunities to let go.

Sleep is one of the greatest opportunities to practise surrendering. My quality of sleep was always correlated with how often I practised surrender. Tossing and turning helped my thoughts to run riot. Alternatively, by choosing to stay still and letting go of the urge to toss and turn, I found my body would sooner or later relax, and eventually, my mind would follow. What helped with sleep was telling myself to 'let go' during the day when I'd notice my body was tense. It meant the anxiety didn't accumulate and erupt just before sleep, at the end of the day.

Surrender also means choosing to trust people. Rather than ask for reassurance or imagine the potential bad scenarios, I'd choose to sit with the feeling that made me want to seek reassurance and observe it. A common example is being in a position where you have to delegate at work and trust that the people in question will complete the work to an acceptable standard. Deciding not to trust people can be no healthier than deciding to hold a grudge. The weight gets carried, and you're the one that becomes burdened. When I've practised surrender, I experienced better psychological well-being and an increased internal locus of control.

If ever a confrontation turned into a 'tit for tat', I would become aware of it and walk away. A common example is calling out one another's hypocrisy. It can sound something like 'but you did that just the other day!' in an argumentative tone. I believe a part of being human is that we will all have degrees of hypocrisy. We need to appreciate the input of trying to abide by good values, in addition to the output of actually abiding by them. Of course, we will slip up. Accepting that will happen to us and to others without judgement is powerful.

Another example is taking things personally. A lesson I continue to learn so often is that a person's behaviour isn't personal but is often a reflection of how they feel about themselves. An example is if someone is very critical of you. It's useful to see how they treat others, as all too often critical people will not just be critical to one person. To acknowledge this about someone means you can justify taking what they say with a pinch of salt. It was clearer to see when I could recognise the same behaviour that I was receiving was also imposed on others; it's not personal.

Surrendering is about being accepting of what is and not trying too hard to control. There is a balance to be struck as with any aspect of life, and you don't want to surrender to the extent that you completely delegate control to an outside force and thereby lack self-control.

Surrender has proved to be most effective for people with addictions. For instance, there is what's known as the Twelve-Step programmes (Kelly, 2017), and surrender is said to be at the heart of those Twelve Steps (The Berkeley Well-Being Institute, n.d.). Addicts are encouraged to surrender and accept their addictive nature is outside of their control. This means accepting that cravings will come rather than try to resist those cravings. It's important to note that surrendering is still a choice in itself. It can be the most energy-conserving option and thereby the most effective.

Reflection question

Do you see yourself as more easy-going or more controlling? What are the ways in which you can make this more balanced in order to benefit your mental health?

Being too controlling would be tiresome and damage your relationship with others, whilst being too easy-going may make you come across as careless, also making your life more difficult in the long run.

14. Dip your toe outside of your comfort zone

What happens if we don't face our fears? Fear controls us. We avoid situations that trigger it. Anxiety controls us. The solution is to choose to face the trigger in small doses, even if that is just through visualisation. What does this look like, specifically? We trigger the emotional blockage, become mindful of it, and sit with it in a safe space rather than avoid it. This is the path to enable its release.

We need growth, which only happens by stepping outside of our comfort zone. Stepping outside of a comfort zone is not going to feel nice at the time. It requires you to have a compassionate relationship with your inner child and have the child's back if it becomes too much and you need to leave the triggering situation. There's no shame in that either. Doing so only builds the trusting relationship you have with yourself, which will reap more confidence in your life. What matters is that it's coming from a place of attempting to face fear rather than running from it.

I actually found that I had stepped too far outside of my comfort zone. I travelled to Australia as a backpacker, ready to stay in hostels and overcome my social anxiety. However, events happened outside of my control that brought on a grief process. Rather than go home back to my roots and ride through this grief process, I continued with my plans of facing my fears.

This would be a poor decision, as my system just became overloaded. Therefore, it is important that if you do plan to face your fears, you're able to put those plans on hold if something difficult happens in the meantime which needs prioritising. Had I taken things more slowly, and even considered visualising doing the trip, the outcome could've been very different. The visualisation would've enabled my subconscious to rehearse what was to come, and so the effect is that the nervous system sees the event as less threatening.

Recent scientific studies say we have to replace trauma response with positive reaction. It's an opportunity to practise gratitude (Erasing Fear & Traumas Based on the Modern Neuroscience of Fear, 2021). For instance, if I was to list three things I was grateful for about my trip to Australia it would be the following: 1) making new friends, 2) walking along beautiful beaches and 3) meeting distant family.

Research says that increased performance is just one of the many reasons stepping out of your comfort zone is important (Wooll, 2022). It also helps you find out your true potential, reach your goals, and live a more fulfilling life.

A six-step visualisation process

1. In a safe and private space, visualise the event to feel the anxiety. Hold the feeling and return back to visualisation when you lose it. Keep diverting awareness to the body. This will be a rehearsal for the mind so that when you do feel this feeling again, it learns that everything is okay so that the body doesn't add any extra tension to what is already present. Don't forget to breathe.

2. List three things that are positive about the event you're fearing. List three more if you feel the need to do so.

3. Accept that this anxiety reaction will continue to happen. But now you have a rehearsal response to manage it. The cause of this anxiety is over-identification with thoughts and the stories your mind repeats, so this is a process of dis-identifying with them. And remember you can always say no to the real event.

4. Practice staying in the present moment as much as you can outside of this 10-minute visualisation exercise, including during the event, so your brain becomes wired for it rather than being wired to worry. You don't worry when present.

5. Set no expectations. Imagine not just the worst-case scenario but whatever is most realistic that might be more emotionally impactful for you. Embrace the triggering feelings. These emotions can be a lot to feel. If so, focus on a point in the body. The most intense point. You may have physical walls in the body that want proof you don't need their protection anymore. They'll want you to eventually face triggering events and let go in these scenarios, so they know they're no longer needed.

6. The goal need not be to face a fear or completely let go of controlling situations. What matters is that you process the underlying emotion. You can't set an end date for this process.

Choosing to surrender during this visualisation enabled me to identify every obstacle that was preventing me from doing what I wanted to do, and so become aware of what needed healing. I would come to recognise that I was fearing the feeling of fear, rather than the event itself.

15. Putting it all together

"God grant me the serenity to accept the things I cannot change, courage to change the things I can, and wisdom to know the difference." - Reinhold Niebuhr

This book represents the course that I have taken in order to progress on my mental health journey. If I compare the versions of myself pre and post this journey, they are two very different people. Fundamentally, I now have self-trust. I have my own back. I don't put energy into a fear of disappointing others, but rather, I put energy into working on myself. I don't look at the world through a lens of pound signs anymore, wishing to save money at every turn. Instead, I try to make decisions that feel right to my gut, irrespective of the monetary value, or lack of monetary value. I found the biggest difference made through living more authentically was finding a new appreciation for time. Even whilst in a job I was pursuing where I was originally burnt out, I was able to change my mindset where I no longer wished the weeks away. That would lead to changes I never could have foreseen. I went from being burnt out in my job, to someone more open, trusting, and excited to try new things. I much prefer the latter way of living.

For what seems a vast majority of those with depression and anxiety, regulating the nervous system can only help improve symptoms at the very least. Being stuck in 'the vicious cycle' sustained with junk food and the attention economy is many people's coping mechanism today for having a dysregulated nervous system. Once we get out of this cycle, the chemical imbalances in brains of those who have mental health illness are more likely to become balanced as the nervous system becomes more regulated. To get out of this cycle, we need more segments in the day where we can just be the observer of our thoughts and feelings. It is in this state we give ourselves permission to exit autopilot mode. It is in this state we can view things with far more clarity and make more well-informed decisions. Activities that enable us to be in this state may entail moving the body, going out in the sunshine, connecting with others, and doing other activities such as painting or reading where you lose track of time. Exchange time spent doomscrolling with any of these activities, since an excess of notifications and multitasking can overstimulate the nervous system.

By increasing our consciousness through these small segments, we have a better chance of acknowledging which habits don't serve us. We can choose which habits we want to let go of and what new ones we'd like to incorporate. As we practise these new habits, the brain responds through neuroplasticity and rewires itself in order to adapt to the change we have planned and are acting upon. Making time to access a higher level of consciousness through meditation makes way for a calmer mind, which will be mirrored in the nervous system. It will allow the body to be more relaxed more consistently. If having difficulty replacing bad habits, it may be useful to understand where they stem from. They could be linked to having an insecure attachment style, which usually would equate to a lack of self-worth. The first step to creating a more secure attachment style for yourself is to be aware that you're not there yet. From there a number of steps can be taken to be more secure, and this may largely show up in the form of re-parenting yourself.

This looks like having a new inner voice that takes charge over your old ‘inner child’ voice.

Through a healthier routine, we can start to have more power over our lives. We have more energy to live more authentically and therefore are able to prioritise who we truly are as opposed to a version of us that society demands. As this happens, watch the societal mask slip away alongside the tiresome symptoms that come with wearing it. The real you can come and start to live your life.

The person I am today compared to a year ago is completely different, as a result of incorporating the knowledge within this book. I have more energy, confidence, and more genuine relationships with friends and family. I am physically more relaxed. I take my time rather than rush things. I no longer have ‘the Sunday night dread’ for what the next week is going to bring, because I live more fully in the present. Of course, I have not reached an endpoint where all is well, and I don’t think there is such a thing. What matters is that we make progress. What matters is that we try to do better than yesterday, and do so in small, incremental steps. Taking on some habits referenced in the book may be the first steps for you to start living with more confidence and energy to not just be more comfortable with yourself, but to actually get to know yourself more. The self beneath the version you tried to be to appease societal demand. The authentic self. It is this self that is far better at making decisions aligned with what's true to you. Aiming to live a truthful version of yourself is where contentment will start to show up.

Resources

FREEBIE 1 - Action plan

I provide a FREEBIE Action Plan template over the next page that comes with hints & tips. The action plan is based on the process within this book and is suggestive rather than instructive. I appreciate this routine is in no way 'one size fits all'. It's just something for the reader to have a go of and amend as they wish.

There are also TWO sets of routine schedules that I include, should you want more than the first set.

FREEBIE 2 - Daily reflection journal

A part of the freebies provided is a 'daily reflection' journal. It asks for three gratitudes and one lesson for the day based on something that went wrong. This way, we don't start becoming blind to the inevitable problems we will face. What matters is that we learn from them.

Habits Set 1

NOTE: The four habits listed below can be done in any order. What matters is that you just implement 1 at a time for a period of 3 weeks, before implementing the next one.

Habit			Week 1	Week 2	Week 3	21 Days done?	If no, number of days to extend for	Extended done	Keep habit	Feel ready for new habit
1	Gratitude list	E.G:-	✓	✓	✓	X	2	✓	✓	✓
2	Mindfulness Meditation									
3	Journaling/Self-talk*									
4	Breathwork									

* I personally prefer to journal. But other's may prefer talking to writing and so talking to the self is just as viable as writing. It may feel awkward at first but that will go away!

Hints and tips

- Use a staggered approach where you only implement 1 at a time otherwise you will feel overwhelmed and it will not be sustainable.
- Do a habit for at least 3 weeks before you add a new one. It's only after 3 weeks that the habit will become part of the autopilot function of the brain.
- Select 1 habit to do first thing in the morning. It's been shown that how you use your first 15 minutes of the day can significantly alter the remainder of your day.
- Remember to have self compassion for the days you don't do your habits! It's the harder days that are opportunity for stronger change in the mind!

Habits Set 2

NOTE: The four habits listed below can be done in any order. What matters is that you just implement 1 at a time for a period of 3 weeks, before implementing the next one.

Habit			Week 1	Week 2	Week 3	21 Days done?	If no, number of days to extend for	Extended done	Keep habit	Feel ready for new habit
5	Exercise	E.G:-	✓	✓	✓	X	2	✓	✓	✓
6	Drink recommended water intake (2.7l for women and 3.7l for men)									
7	Limit social media time (e.g. to 30 minutes a day)									
8	Take your vitamins (Vitamin B12 and D are said to be common causes of depression)									

FREEBIE 2 - Daily reflection template

One thing that went wrong today was:

What I learnt from this was:

Three things I am grateful for today are…

1. ________________________________

2. ________________________________

3. ________________________________

Three things I want to achieve tomorrow are…

1. ________________________________

2. ________________________________

3. ________________________________

Bibliography

Apa.org. (2021). Mindfulness meditation: A research-proven way to reduce stress. [online] Available at https://www.apa.org/topics/mindfulness/meditation#:~:text=Researchers%20reviewed%20mo re%20than%20200.

Arnsten, A., Mazure, C.M. and Sinha, R. (2012). Neural circuits responsible for conscious self-control are highly vulnerable to even mild stress. When they shut down, primal impulses go unchecked and mental paralysis sets in. *Scientific American*, [online] 306(4), pp.48–53. Available at: https://www.ncbi.nlm.nih.gov/pmc/articles/PMC4774859/.

Brown, J. and Wong, J. (2017). How Gratitude Changes You and Your Brain. [online] Greater Good. Available at: https://greatergood.berkeley.edu/article/item/how_gratitude_changes_you_and_your_brain.

Cleveland Clinic (2019). *What Happens to Your Body During the Fight or Flight Response?* [online] Health Essentials from Cleveland Clinic. Available at: https://health.clevelandclinic.org/what-happens-to-your-body-during-the-fight-or-flight-respo nse/.

Culture. (2013). The Bigger Brains of London Taxi Drivers. [online] Available at: https://www.nationalgeographic.com/culture/article/the-bigger-brains-of-london-taxi-drivers#:~:text=The%20part%20of%20the%20brain [Accessed 14 Mar. 2023].

Debbie Hampton (2019). How Neuroplasticity Changes Over Your Brain's Lifetime. [online] The Best Brain Possible. Available at: https://thebestbrainpossible.com/neuroplasticity-brain-changes-baby/#:~:text=Because%20of%20neuroplasticity%2C%20you%20are [Accessed 14 Mar. 2023].

Döring, A.K. and Knafo-Noam, A. (2019). How Do Our Values Guide Us in Life? Frontiers for Young Minds, 7. doi:https://doi.org/10.3389/frym.2019.00115.

Elliott, A. (2022). *Attachment Theory*. [online] The Child Psychology Service. Available at: https://thechildpsychologyservice.co.uk/theory-article/attachment-theory/

Erasing Fear & Traumas Based On The Modern Neuroscience Of Fear (2021). [Podcast] Huberman Lab. 14 Dec. Available at: https://podcastnotes.org/huberman-lab/episode-49-erasing-fear-traumas-based-on-the-modern-neuroscience-of-fear-huberman-lab/ [Accessed 14 Mar. 2023].

First Things First (2018). *Brain Development - First Things First.* [online] First Things First. Available at: https://www.firstthingsfirst.org/early-childhood-matters/brain-development/.

Healthline. (2021). *Can Shaking Help You Heal Stress and Trauma? Some Experts Say Yes.* [online] Available at: https://www.healthline.com/health/mental-health/can-shaking-your-body-heal-stress-and-trau ma#.

Greater Good. (n.d.). *How Journaling Can Help You in Hard Times.* [online] Available at: https://greatergood.berkeley.edu/article/item/how_journaling_can_help_you_in_hard_times#:~:text=The%20people%20who%20journaled%20saw.

Healthline. (2017). *First Seven Years of Childhood: Are They the Most Important?* [online] Available at: https://www.healthline.com/health/parenting/first-seven-years-of-childhood#By-the-age-of-7.

Johns Hopkins Medicine (2019). *Forgiveness: Your Health Depends on It.* [online] Johns Hopkins Medicine. Available at: https://www.hopkinsmedicine.org/health/wellness-and-prevention/forgiveness-your-health-de pends-on-it.

Learning, L. and Lang, D. (2020). 1950s: Harlow, Bowlby, and Ainsworth. iastate.pressbooks.pub. [online] Available at: https://iastate.pressbooks.pub/parentingfamilydiversity/chapter/bowlby-ainsworth/#:~:text=B uilding%20on%20the%20work%20of.

Lenroot, R.K. and Giedd, J.N. (2008). The changing impact of genes and environment on brain development during childhood and adolescence: Initial findings from a neuroimaging study of pediatric twins. *Development and Psychopathology*, 20(4), pp.1161 1175.

MindHealth360. (n.d.). *Nervous system dysregulation.* [online] Available at: https://www.mindhealth360.com/contributor/nervous-system-dysregulation/#:~:text=When% 20we%20talk%20of%20a [Accessed 11 Nov. 2022].

Mental Health Foundation (2022). *People seeking help: statistics.* [online] www.mentalhealth.org.uk. Available at: https://www.mentalhealth.org.uk/explore-mental-health/mental-health-statistics/people-seekin g-help-statistics.

Millman, D. (2010). Body Mind Mastery. New World Library.

Mi-Psych | Mindfulness & Clinical Psychology Solutions. (2017). Your Brain's 3 Emotion Regulation Systems | Learn to Soothe Yourself. [online] Available at: https://mi-psych.com.au/your-brains-3-emotion-regulation-systems/.

Newman, K.M. (2020). How Journaling Can Help You in Hard Times. [online] Greater Good. Available at: https://greatergood.berkeley.edu/article/item/how_journaling_can_help_you_in_hard_times.

ResearchGate. (n.d.). *(PDF) Acute Changes in Autonomic Nerve Activity during Passive Static Stretching*. [online] Available at: https://www.researchgate.net/publication/274517864_Acute_Changes_in_Autonomic_Nerve_Activity_during_Passive_Static_Stretching.

Singh, M. (2019). *NPR Choice page*. [online] Npr.org. Available at: https://www.npr.org/sections/health-shots/2018/12/24/678232331/if-you-feel-thankful-write-i t-down-its-good-for-your-health.

Soumyaranjan Nayak (2017). *Does Music Help You Focus Better On Work?* [online] Toppr Bytes. Available at: https://www.toppr.com/bytes/music-help-focus/.

The Berkeley Well-Being Institute. (n.d.). Surrendering: Definition, Meditations, & Quotes. [online] Available at: https://www.berkeleywellbeing.com/surrendering.html.

The Holistic Psychologist. (2018). *Vagus Nerve: A Path to Healing*. [online] Available at: https://theholisticpsychologist.com/vagus_nerve_a_path-to-healing/.

The Holistic Psychologist. (n.d.). *The New Science Archives*. [online] Available at: https://theholisticpsychologist.com/category/the-new-science/ [Accessed 11 Nov. 2022].

The Oklahoman. (n.d.). Strange but true: 95 percent of brain activity is unconscious. [online] Available at: https://eu.oklahoman.com/story/lifestyle/2018/10/09/strange-but-true-95-percent-of-brain-activity-is-unconscious/60496296007/#:~:text=Current%20scientific%20estimates%20are%20th at [Accessed 14 Mar. 2023]

Third Space. (2021). *The Science Behind Positive Affirmations*. [online] Available at: https://www.thirdspace.london/this-space/2021/02/the-science-behind-positive-affirmations/.

Wooll, M. (2022). How to get out of your comfort zone (in 6 simple steps). BetterUp. [online] 11 Mar. Available at: https://www.betterup.com/blog/comfort-zone.

World Health Organization (2022). *Mental disorders*. [online] Who.int. Available at: https://www.who.int/news-room/fact-sheets/detail/mental-disorders.

WPH Physio. (2021). *Tired At Work? Reduce Fatigue With Deep Breathing Exercises*. [online] Available at: https://wphphysio.com.au/why-are-desk-workers-so-tired/ [Accessed 23 Apr. 2022].

www.medicalnewstoday.com. (2021). *Amygdala hijack: Symptoms, causes, and prevention*. [online] Available at: https://www.medicalnewstoday.com/articles/amygdala-hijack#:~:text=Fight%2Dor%2Dflight%20as%20a%20response%20to%20a%20threat&text=When%20a%20person%20feels%20st ressed [Accessed 23 Apr. 2022].)

www.england.nhs.uk. (n.d.). *NHS England» Take your health seriously*. [online] Available at: https://www.england.nhs.uk/blog/take-your-health-seriously/#:~:text=On%20sympathetic%20nervous%20system%20overdrive [Accessed 9 Jan. 2023].

www.google.com. (n.d.). *mindfulness meditation statistics - Google Search*. [online] Available at: https://www.google.com/search?q=mindfulness+meditation+statistics&rlz=1CAPGTQ_enGB1039GB1039&oq=mindfulness+meditation+statistic&aqs=chrome.0.0i512j69i57j0i390l4.7633j0j4&sourceid=chrome&ie=UTF-8 [Accessed 9 Jan. 2023]

The Berkeley Well-Being Institute. (n.d.). *Surrendering: Definition, Meditations, & Quotes*. [online] Available at: https://www.berkeleywellbeing.com/surrendering.html [Accessed 9 Jan. 2023].

www.betterup.com. (n.d.). *How to get out of your comfort zone (in 6 simple steps)*. [online] Available at: https://www.betterup.com/blog/comfortzone#:~:text=The%20best%20way%20to%20leave.

www.bbc.co.uk. (n.d.). House of Maxwell. [online] Available at: https://www.bbc.co.uk/iplayer/episodes/p0b64j3y/house-of-maxwell [Accessed 14 Mar. 2023].

www.mentalhealth.org.uk. (n.d.). Family and parenting: statistics. [online] Available at: https://www.mentalhealth.org.uk/explore-mental-health/statistics/family-parenting-statistics#:~:text=Approximately%2068%25%20of%20women%20and.happify.com. (n.d.). 5 Scientific Facts that Prove Gratitude is Good for You. [online] Available at: https://www.happify.com/hd/5-scientific-facts-that-prove-gratitude-is-good-for-you/.

Toussaint, L.L., Shields, G.S. and Slavich, G.M. (2016). Forgiveness, Stress, and Health: a 5-Week Dynamic Parallel Process Study. Annals of Behavioral Medicine, [online] 50(5), pp.727–735. doi:https://doi.org/10.1007/s12160-016-9796-6.

www.psychologytoday.com. (n.d.). 6 Important Facts About Forgiveness | Psychology Today. [online] Available at: https://www.psychologytoday.com/us/blog/the-mindful-self-express/201506/6-important-fact s-about-forgiveness

Walker, R. (2019). Stressed Brits buy record number of self-help books. [online] The Guardian. Available at: https://www.theguardian.com/books/2019/mar/09/self-help-books-sstressed-brits-buy-record- number.

Williams, M. and Penman, D. (2011). Mindfulness. Hachette UK.

Yoon, K.L. and Zinbarg, R.E. (2008). Interpreting neutral faces as threatening is a default mode for socially anxious individuals. Journal of Abnormal Psychology, 117(3), pp.680–685. doi:https://doi.org/10.1037/0021-843x.117.3.680.

Acknowledgements

This book would not have been possible without the input from Paper Raven Books. Thanks also to my parents for always being supportive in what I do.

RG

About the author

Rachel George completed a 2:1 in BSc Accountancy and would go on to complete professional exams to qualify as a chartered accountant. At this stage Rachel took a career break and would go backpacking to Australia. It was during this career break that Rachel committed to this writing. Rachel utilised knowledge about mental health from her own research, in addition to her own personal experiences.

Printed in Great Britain
by Amazon

5462ee4c-b7e1-4823-ae6e-4d0a59ee2403R01